M000079331

31 Words to
Create a Guilt-Free Life

31 Words to
Create a Guilt-Free Life

Finding the Freedom to Be Your Most Powerful Self

A Simple Guide to Self-Care, Balance, and Joy

EDITED BY
KAREN BOURIS

INNER OCEAN PUBLISHING
Maui · San Francisco

Inner Ocean Publishing, Inc.
P.O. Box 1239
Makawao, Maui, HI 96768-1239
www.innerocean.com

Cover and book design by Yoori Kim

Inner Ocean Publishing is a member of Green Press Initiative, a nonprofit
program dedicated to supporting publishers in their efforts to reduce their use
of fiber sourced from endangered forests. We elected to print this title on 50%
postconsumer recycled paper with the recycled portion processed chlorine free. As
a result, we have saved the following resources: 433 trees, 428,515 lbs of solid
waste, 3,669,747 gallons of water, 1,157,374 lbs of net greenhouse gases, 7,492
million BTU's (Source: Environmental Defense Paper Calculator). For more
information on the Green Press Initiative, visit
http://www.greenpressinitiative.org.

PUBLISHER CATALOGING-IN-PUBLICATION DATA
    31 words to create a guilt-free life : finding the freedom to be your most
    powerful self : a simple guide to self-care, balance, and joy / edited by
    Karen Bouris. — Maui : Inner Ocean, 2006.
        p. ; cm.
    ISBN-13: 978-1-973022-59-6 (pbk.)
    ISBN-10: 1-973022-59-1 (pbk.)
    Offers anecdotes with corresponding exercises on how to banish your inner
    critic, balance your needs with those of others, and clear the way to reaching
    your ultimate potential.
1. Self-actualization (Psychology) 2. Self-esteem. 3. Self-help techniques.
I. Bouris, Karen. II. Thirty-one words to create a guilt-free life. III. Create a
guilt-free life.
    BF637.S4 T45 2006
    158.1—dc22   0606

Printed in the United States of America
05 06 07 08 09 10 DATA 10 9 8 7 6 5 4 3 2 1

DISTRIBUTED BY PUBLISHER'S GROUP WEST
For information on promotions, bulk purchases, premiums, or educational use,
please contact: 866.731.2216 or sales@innerocean.com.

Introduction by Karen Bouris, Editor   ix

SECTION I
Self-Care

Honesty
Acknowledging Your True Feelings   2

Forgiveness
Experiencing the Grace of Letting Go   5

Space
Claiming Your Right to Breathe   8

Generosity
Giving from the Heart Instead of the Head   11

Kindness
Learning to Befriend Yourself   14

Nurturance
Becoming Your Own Loving Parent   17

Gratitude
Giving Thanks for It All   20

Reality
Accepting Things as They Are Right Now   23

Soothing
Finding Your Way to a Place of Calm   26

Integrity
Strengthening Your Backbone   29

Balance

Recognition
Seeing Guilt for What It Really Is   34

Action
Owning Up to the Pain You've Caused   37

Acceptance
Coming to Terms with Realistic Expectations   40

Compassion
Fostering Care Instead of Guilt   43

Communication
Speaking Up for Your Right to Be Guilt-Free   46

Connection
Breaking the Silence of Guilt and Shame   49

Love
Achieving Balanced Maturity   52

Responsibility
Getting Rid of Flakiness Guilt   55

Appreciation
Breaking the Cycle of Criticism   58

Transformation
Moving from Guilt to Peace   61

Joy

Passion
Nurturing Your Gifts   66

Pleasure
Allowing Life to Feel Good   69

Focus
Living in the Moment   72

Independence
Practicing Going Solo   75

Poise
Transforming Guilt to Grace   78

Motivation
Finding the Wind for Your Sales   81

Individuality
Being Your Most Powerful Self   84

Energy
Replenishing the Soul   87

Delight
Noticing the Little Things   90

Freedom
Breaking Away to Find the Right Home   93

Innocence
Relishing the Absence of Guilt   96

Introduction

Yes, I'm guilty of feeling guilty.

I feel guilty for being born in a country of such privilege. I feel guilty for living in Hawaii—I mean, it's paradise, for crying out loud. I feel remorse for being mean to Lisa in sixth grade and saying cruel things about Leanne in high school. I feel inadequate and shameful that I don't send my kids' grandparents more photos. Or any photos really. When at work I feel pangs of guilt and conflicted for not spending enough time with my children, and when I'm with my kids, I feel terrible for not giving enough to my job. As a mother who regularly does not volunteer at my kids' school, I feel guilty. Not to mention my contrition about not being involved in more community service projects in my area.

Heaped on top of all this is the guilt I feel for *feeling guilty*. Who am I to suffer or complain, when by all rights I should have nothing of real consequence to complain about? When I watch the news or read a newspaper, I worry that I'm not doing more to change the world and relieve all the suffering people are enduring. Bottom line: All of this guilt weighs on me like a full-time job.

A wise friend recently listened to me catalog my crushing guilt. And after listening patiently she said, "You know, guilt is a form of ingratitude."

Wow. The truth of her comment stopped me in my tracks. Her words rang true and strong, and I heard them loud and clear.

Instead of feeling grateful for everything that's good in my life, I instead misuse them to fuel my self-flagellating guilt. Rather than wasting my time feeling undeserving of whatever good cards I've been dealt, I could be nourishing myself with gratitude. From the safe, solid footing of gratitude, wouldn't we all have a better chance to find our mission in life and do meaningful things in the world?

Ultimately, our guilt does not serve anyone. It does not enrich us or those around us. It does not relieve suffering or create change. It does not make us better, more empathetic people. Guilt is not a morally upstanding emotion, though we often trick ourselves into thinking it is. In reality, all it does is drain our energy for giving genuine love, compassion, and support to ourselves, our immediate families, and our human family.

Guilt is pervasive, assuming many forms. It convinces us that we need it to be good and loving. And it hides in all our dark places. So in order to truly eradicate guilt, burdensome and counterproductive beast that it is, we have to pull the skeletons out of the closet, examine them with thoughtfulness and honesty and love, release them. From there, we can allow genuine care and compassion to fuel us to make the changes in our lives and in our world.

So how exactly can 31 *words* help us?

A single word can invoke myriad reactions: Vacation. Parents. Graduation. Funeral. Breeze. Wedding. Birth.

Or more potently: Rwanda. Tsunami. Katrina. Bombs.

And perhaps closer to home: Obligation. Mortgage. Child care. Unemployment. Anger. Gratitude. Love. Conflict.

Guilt. Release. Peace.

Last year, my New Year's resolutions consisted of one word

(albeit a hyphenated one): self-care. I said it many, many times, jokingly at first, because I was so uncomfortable with making self-care a priority that I had to say it tongue-in-cheek. Eventually, though, with all that repeating, the jokiness started to dissipate and the true calling of that word began to permeate my being. Decisions were made measured by the self-care ruler. Does this support my emotional and physical health and happiness? Self-care. The word became my mantra, and it allowed my decision making to become less guilt inducing each time.

Once you realize the power of a single word, you start to add a few more to the repertoire. With my children, I focus on two words: compassion and gratitude. We try to have compassion for all creatures, from the cockroaches to the bats, from the rats in the banana trees to the worms in the bananas. (As yet, I have been unable to extend compassion to the centipedes.) At dinner we say a blessing of gratitude, for the farmers who grew the food on the table and the animals who gave up their lives to feed us. We express gratitude for our majestic and vital natural environment, and the rich group of friends and family in our lives. Compassion and gratitude.

Collectively, the editors in our office have selected, researched, and written about 31 separate words that can support a guilt-free existence. And since a month is generally thirty-one days, we wanted to give a month's worth of word power.

The first section of this book is all about "Self-Care," since living guilt-free means practicing self-care, first and foremost. We all have to start by getting right with ourselves before we can healthily and happily connect and extend to others.

The second section focuses on living in balance, connecting with others from a place of love instead of from a place of obligation and reproach. We all battle feelings of guilt daily, regarding loved ones and strangers alike; so balancing the needs of ourselves with the needs of others is explored in Section II.

And, thankfully, living guilt-free means finally being able to fully embrace joy and our own personal missions in the world. This is the fun part, but it's all too easy to lose touch with our sense of joy, pleasure, freedom, and fun when we're inundated with guilt. Section III[or three, if change above] is designed to help you come back to a place of poised independence and experience delight in your life and your relationships.

Once you are living guilt-free—imagine, *guilt-free!*—you can be your most powerful self. You can be a spectacular visionary, influence your loved ones and community members with your light, and step into your rightful space as the strong, vital individual you are meant to be.

—*March 2006, Maui, Hawaii*

"Our deepest fear is not that we are inadequate. Our deepest fear is that we powerful beyond measure. It is our Light, not our Darkness, that most frightens us. We ask ourselves, who am I to be brilliant, gorgeous, talented, fabulous? Actually, who are you not to be?

—MARIANNE WILLIAMSON, *A Return to Love*

Self-Care

Honesty

We all know guilt isn't good. It doesn't make us better friends, partners, or parents. It's not motivating, it's depleting. It's not heroic, it's tragic. It's a destructive form of self-flagellation that consumes our energy and leaves us more distanced from the people we love. So why would we ever want to cop to such a regressive, disempowering emotion? Isn't it better to hide it away in a dark little corner of our hearts and pretend we're above it? Shouldn't we just suck it up and be closeted guilt cases?

In short, no way.

Here's the honest, radical truth: Each of your feelings, no matter how unacceptable or unhelpful they seem, deserves nothing less than your complete love and attention. But how can you tend to something you won't consciously acknowledge? (You can't.) How can you expect to be guilt-free without wading through all of that creepy, crawly guilt? (Same answer.)

Let's get completely honest about guilt. Start paying attention to when and why you feel it. Brad Blanton, author of *Radical Honesty: How to Transform Your Life by Telling the Truth,* suggests a way to identify your guilt, "Notice the bodily sensations associated with what you have called guilt (feeling constricted in your breathing, cowering, feeling tense, frowning)."

Once you notice those sensations, name your emotion, at least to yourself: "Oh, here's that cringy feeling again. I feel guilty." You'll be surprised how honestly naming your true feelings will free you. It's a powerful start to living a guilt-free life.

EXERCISE

Blanton proposes that when someone does or says something that makes us feel guilty, we inevitably feel resentful. His ultimate recommendation is to express that resentment ("I resent you for XX"), engaging in an open exchange of resentments until both parties can honestly complete the phrase "I appreciate you for XX." He believes that whether or not our feelings are rational, it's important to get them out there so they can be resolved.

Although refreshing, Blanton's idea is perhaps not entirely realistic. For instance, it isn't appropriate to tell your kids or your boss you resent them (even though you sometimes do) and expect that they'll be capable or willing to engage in this kind of clearing process. But that doesn't mean you can't be honest with *yourself* about your guilt and corresponding resentment. In fact, it's crucial that you are.

To that end, get yourself a blank notebook and start your own guilt and resentment log. Divide it into three columns: In the first, complete the sentence, "I feel guilty about XX"; in the second, describe the physical sensations of your guilt; and in the third, complete the sentence, "I resent XX for XX." Let yourself be completely, wonderfully honest, and give yourself a few minutes to focus on and acknowledge those uncomfortable feelings. When allowed to run its course, instead of being stuffed and ignored, your guilt will begin to dissolve and float away.

I love and accept myself with all of
my guilty feelings.

Forgiveness

In her book *All About Love,* author and cultural critic bell hooks writes about the power of forgiveness: "Forgiveness is an act of generosity. It requires that we place releasing someone else from the prison of their guilt or anguish over our feelings of outrage or anger. By forgiving we clear a path on the way to love."

Forgiving is viewed in our culture as a noble act that serves the greater good. As hooks so powerfully says, forgiveness makes way for love. Why, then, does self-forgiveness feel selfish? Why do we instead imprison ourselves in fortresses of guilt and shame? Has self-punishment ever *actually* righted any of your real or imagined wrongdoings?

Rachel's brand of kindness to others involved a good deal of holding her own feet to the fire. If she slipped up, even if it was unintentional, she wouldn't forgive herself. To her, feeling guilty and ashamed meant she was making amends.

Recently, Rachel invited a new coworker to lunch, and he happily agreed. After they sat down, she rushed to break the awkward silence. Noticing his wedding band, she blurted, "So, how long have you and your wife been married?" He looked at his band and smiled, "Actually, my partner is a man. We've been together for eight years."

Rachel felt terrible about her assumption. She apologized immediately, and he smiled and said, "No problem." She cringed with shame and could barely follow the conversation during the rest of the lunch.

She felt guilty all day. She had meant well, but she couldn't allow herself to find comfort in that. She was about to take her miserable self home when he stopped by her office. "Hey," he said warmly, "Thank you again for lunch. I really enjoyed it." He'd clearly forgiven her. He knew she hadn't been intentionally hurtful by her heartfelt apology. He'd let it go. Why couldn't she?

That night she had dinner with a friend, who listened sympathetically before offering something she'd heard from a wise teacher: "Imagine putting your head into the mouth of the dragon and feeling comfortable there." In Rachel's case, this meant putting her head in the dragon of her guilt, shame, and embarrassment, laying her head ever so softly into the dragon's mouth and breathing deeply into these feelings.

The dragon of painful feelings—guilt, shame, regret, humiliation, loneliness, grief, rejection, loss—can be dark, and all-powerful (especially at 4:00 a.m.). But when you breathe into these feelings and forgive yourself, you remember that you are okay. Now there's a noble thought.

Bring to mind something you haven't forgiven yourself for. Close your eyes and imagine putting your head into the mouth of that dragon. Remember what you did and said, and how it was hurtful. Breathe into that pain and stop letting it rule your feelings of self-worth. Be completely honest about your mistake, and ask yourself for forgiveness. Imagine your wiser self emerging and replying, with love and under-standing, "I forgive you." Become intimate with your dragons and extinguish their fires.

I forgive my mistakes and feel at peace with myself.

Space

Lucia prided herself on being the best mom to her two daughters, the most loving partner, and the most innovative employee. She pushed herself from dawn till dusk. Though chronically exhausted, she felt like she had it all and then some.

That is, until the day she woke up with a pain in her abdomen, but still got up, got her kids ready for school, loaded the dishwasher, picked up everyone in her carpool, and drove to work. The pain worsened, but Lucia convinced herself it would pass. She had a presentation to give and she wasn't about to miss it for an upset stomach. Until she passed out and was rushed to the hospital.

To her surprise, her weeklong stay in the hospital became a rejuvenating experience, sans daily demands. She luxuriated in a bed to herself and compassionate nurses who didn't require anything from her. As she soaked in the relative peace and quiet, she felt she was coming back to herself. She'd forgotten what it was like to read a book without interruption, to listen to her own thoughts and dreams for a change. By the end of the week, she'd made a radical new promise to herself: She'd make sure she had some time to herself every week.

Prevention is everything. If you make space for yourself before you fall into depression, give up on your relationship, yell at your kids, or quit your job, you may be able to salvage the things that are important to you. But sometimes the guilt feels so much more pressing. When we believe that everyone else should come first, we feel horrible guilt when we desire time for ourselves.

In *Codependent No More,* Melody Beattie talks about detachment as a way to release guilt. "Detachment does not mean we don't care. It means we learn to love, care, and be involved without going crazy."

Skeptical? Then consider this: Beattie suggests that the way to best recognize when we need to detach is to *identify every instance in which it seems impossible to do so*, because that's where we need it most. Don't wait to fall ill and get hospitalized to have your own rest cure. Create space for yourself—today.

 EXERCISE

If life feels crowded, free yourself by acknowledging that this is of your own doing. Schedule time for yourself first, above all else. Start with a minimum of thirty minutes each day. Write in your journal what it is you want to do—whether it's napping, exercising, reading in the bath, or sipping tea in your favorite café. Whenever you start to feel guilty, take one minute to articulate why, and then, in your most nurturing internal voice, repeat to yourself, "That is very important to me, and so is taking this space for myself. This space is crucial to my ability to care for myself and others." Then return to your space, take a nice deep breath, and allow yourself to enjoy.

I regularly take space for myself, which benefits me and everyone I love.

Generosity

Generosity is a tricky concept, one that comes with a hair-pin trigger for guilt. Whenever we are asked for a favor, or we see someone else who needs or wants something they aren't getting, we have to make a decision: Will I help or not? These decisions are complicated, though we're usually required to make them instantly. If we say no, we may be met with an onslaught of guilt. Some of us are so afraid to feel those feelings that we say "yes" every time, regardless of whether or not it's something we genuinely want to—or can—give.

Giving in order to avoid guilt is not truly generous. Generosity isn't just about action; it's about a quality of spirit, a genuine willingness to give. If you barely remember how to say the word "no," chances are that you've lost touch with your true generosity. If you feel unappreciated for all that you do, you're not giving from a place of willing generosity.

Taking an action simply to avoid a painful emotion is not a genuine way to live. It's an unfortunate tradeoff. And living disingenuously leads to other painful emotions—like depression, anxiety, resentment, and bitterness. Giving from the heart instead of the head is imperative.

Everyone can be selfish. Sometimes we want the last piece, the best seat, or the first place in line. It's human desire, and *it's not a bad thing*. Allowing ourselves to have something we want is an act of generosity toward ourselves. It's only when we start giving all of our time or resources to others and neglect ourselves that we become a miser.

How do we avoid being a martyr, sacrificing so much of ourselves that there's not much of a self left, and being a miser, hoarding so much that we neglect to care for our loved ones and communities? The trick is to look inward and make honest decisions about when to give to ourselves and to others based on what feels expansive, invigorating, grounding, and deeply fulfilling.

EXERCISE

For one day, make a list of every little thing requested of you by yourself and others. Next to this list, note whether you said "yes" or "no," as well as what you wanted to say to the request. If you aren't sure, check your physical self. When your chest or throat tightens, or your heart starts pounding, or you can't help but sigh, you probably want to say "no." When you feel energized by the request, or openhearted and connected to the person making the request, it's more likely that "yes" is your honest answer. At the end of the day, take a look at your sheet, and note how often you're going with or against your true generosity. While we sometimes have to do things we don't want, getting conscious about when we do so is the first step to genuine generosity.

I am generous to myself and others, always giving what I genuinely want to give.

Kindness

For many of us, the idea of being a kind friend to ourselves is a foreign concept that can seem elusive, or even greedy or self-indulgent. But the truth is, being kind to ourselves is an incredibly generous act that supports us in bestowing kindness to others. It's a powerful way to change the world from the inside out, not to mention that it just plain feels good.

In her book *Lovingkindness*, Sharon Saltzberg discusses the Buddhist take on kindness, "The practice of metta, uncovering the force of love that can uproot fear, anger, and guilt, begins with befriending ourselves. The foundation of metta practice is to know how to be our own friend. According to the Buddha, 'You can search throughout the entire universe for someone who is more deserving of your love and affection than you are yourself, and that person is not to be found anywhere. You yourself, as much as anybody in the entire universe, deserve your love and affection.'"

How might your day have been different if you approached it from the place of being your own kind, loving friend? But learning how to befriend yourself doesn't just happen instantaneously—it takes practice. You need to get to know your own true feelings and needs, and build inner-trust by taking steps to honor and address them. You need to prove to yourself over time that you won't consistently let yourself down by rejecting or abandoning yourself (and that, on the times when you do fail yourself, you can apologize and renew your commitment to yourself). Building this friendship takes time, but the relationship you'll build will be the most important and influential one of your lifetime.

EXERCISE Write down some of the nicest things other people have done for you. Maybe your sweetheart comforted you when you were overwhelmed, or your coworker spoke up to make sure you got credit for a great idea, or a stranger complimented you on something you were wearing. Revel in these memories of kind words, generous gestures, and unexpected compliments, and record them in vivid detail, including how they made you feel physically and emotionally. Then, with the same pleasure and leisure, write down the kindest things you've done for family members, friends, and strangers. Allow the good feelings of doing something kind to fill you.

Once you've got a nice long list and you're basking in the memory of all of this kindness, write a generous list of kind things you could do for yourself every day this month. Include both quick things (such as giving yourself compliments and kudos) and things that take longer (like letting yourself sleep in on a weekend, even if there's too much to do). Try bestowing kindness on yourself every day for a month and see how it begins to buoy your spirits and inspire you to act kindly to others from a genuine place of good feeling, rather than from a place of guilty "shoulds."

Every day I shower myself with loving kindness.

Nurturance

When we think of nurturing, many of us think first of a loving parent tending to a child. Once we're adults, we may assume we don't need or deserve any more nurturing. If we crave it, we may feel we're being immature. We're all too often told to grow up, keep a stiff upper lip, stick it out.

That's certainly not the most nourishing existence we can choose for ourselves. Self-neglect allows our painful feelings to flourish. Guilt, shame, fear, anxiety, and depression pop up everywhere, and somehow we're led to think that the mature, adult thing to do is to suck it up—when what we really need to do is tend to our spirit.

Our brilliant therapist friend Seana offered another view of nurturing that encourages us to tend to all the parts of ourselves, "Whenever you're feeling anxiety, horrible guilt, fear, this is your scared kid. And you need to ask yourself, what would that kid need? What can I—the powerful, healthy adult—do to take care of that kid and these emotions that can come back so quickly?"

For many of us, the term "inner child" can trigger 1970s flashbacks or seem self-indulgent. It's important to distinguish between being childish and childlike. There's a part of all of us that's a sweet, playful, creative, and sometimes frightened kid. When neglected—when we shelve our feelings and needs and put others first to avoid feeling guilty for taking care of ourselves—the part of ourselves that's childlike feels sad, lonely, depressed, angry, and hopeless, which can lead to internal conflicts that result in self-sabotaging behaviors and chronic painful emotions.

In *Self-Parenting: The Complete Guide to Inner Conversations,* John K. Pollard suggests that if we spend time each day asking our inner children how they feel, what they enjoy, and what isn't working for them, we can resolve the inner conflicts that keep us from releasing painful feelings and moving forward in our lives unencumbered. Through breaking through the taboo and adequately nurturing ourselves, we can move that much closer to living a guilt-free life.

Like a garden, our internal selves need consistent and regular nurturance. In the same way that you can't water your garden once and consider it done, tending to your own needs and feelings is an ongoing endeavor. Why not start growing your beautiful garden today? Grab a notebook and ask the child inside you "How are you feeling today?" "What do you need?" and "How can I help you?" Allow that child inside to write down answers to these questions honestly, knowing that you will respond with love and understanding, and that your intention is to be caring and helpful. It might feel awkward at first, but these kinds of interactions can help you get in touch with your tender, vulnerable side so that you can heal your deepest wounds and release your greatest creativity and vitality.

I am a loving, caring, encouraging parent
to my child self.

Gratitude

We all have our share of pain and regrets. We are weighted with resentment and guilt for everything hurtful that we've done and that's been done to us. Are you ready to move forward less encumbered by this heavy burden?

Jack's mom was the Queen of Guilt. When he played football, went to an out-of-state college, decided to pursue a career of his own choosing, and got engaged against his mother's wishes, she droned, "How could you do this to *me?*" Each time, he picked up a bag of resentment and guilt. Eventually, Jack became crippled by his emotional baggage.

While in therapy, Jack realized that his anger and resentment toward his mother wasn't doing him any good. His therapist suggested he consider what positive attributes he'd developed as a response to the guilt, and to feel *grateful*— that's right, *grateful*—for how his mother's problematic behavior had helped to shape him into the person he'd become. Jack resisted the idea. He didn't want to give his mother any credit.

In *Gratitude: A Way of Life*, Louise L. Hay addresses this, "Unconditional gratitude given in these situations may at first feel as if we are letting people we dislike 'off the hook.' I can assure you from my own experience that it is ourselves we are letting off the hook. Gratitude, like its sister, forgiveness, frees the giver first of all. Gratitude brings freedom to our self-imposed prison of hatred and revenge."

Jack had to learn that he wasn't expressing gratitude to his mom, he was finding gratitude within himself for himself. He was recognizing that his mother's incessant guilt-tripping had resulted in his being independent in the face of disapproval and clear about his own desires. Eventually, he was able to let go of his mother's guilt, while maintaining a sense of gratitude for where her guilt had led him.

EXERCISE

Hay offers excellent parameters on to facilitate gratitude while remaining true to yourself: "It's important that you be honest with your feelings and not block out old hurts or pretend everything is all right if it isn't. To see the spiritual gift of painful experiences, I release my ideas of how I want things to be. It helps to ask questions of myself such as, 'How did this person help me become more aware of my spiritual nature? How did their action lead me or push me in a particular direction that benefited my spiritual growth? Even if the action was deemed harmful to my human and physical being, how did this action enhance and support my spiritual being?'"

Think back to the single most harmful thing someone has ever done to you. Using Hay's guidelines for self-inquiry, allow your heart to see how the pains of the past have allowed you to become your beautiful self. Focus on feeling grateful and accepting, for every single moment of your life, which has led you to where you are right now.

I feel gratitude for everything that has led up to this moment; it has all made me a wonderful and unique person.

Reality

Marco was the family success story. He'd done well in school, went to college and law school, and got a good job at a corporate law firm. He made more money than his mom and dad combined, which thrilled them. They'd made many sacrifices for their two sons, both working two jobs at times to help pay for tutoring and summer classes, and they were thrilled at how well Marco had done. Now if only José would follow in his brother's footsteps. But here he was, nineteen, no plans for college, still living at home, and working as a hotdog vendor at the ballpark.

Every Sunday when Marco came for dinner Marco's parents would go shower him with praise, and then, inevitably, they'd turn to José and ask him what his future plans were. José would get angry and defensive and storm out, his parents would get hurt and even more worried about their son, and Marco would feel wracked with guilt, as if it were up to him to save his little brother and please his parents. Marco sensed he'd never be able to feel satisfied with his life until José was successful, too.

Marco offered to pay José's expenses for local junior college. But soon José dropped out, saying school interfered with his job. Marco said he'd give José money so he could quit, but José liked his job and didn't want to quit.

Marco had to accept that José wasn't interested in school. José seemed genuinely happy at his job, even though it wasn't what their parents or Marco thought of as a successful career. José liked being out in the sunshine with the crowd—that was who he was.

According to *Mindfulness and Acceptance*, edited by Steven C. Hayes, et al, "The practice of acceptance includes focusing on the current moment, seeing reality as it is without 'delusions,' and accepting reality without judgment … Acceptance is experiencing something without the haze of what one wants and does not want it to be. It is the unrivaled entering into reality as it exists."

Marco had to face his guilt about José, and not judge him because he made less money. Marco finally accepted that José had made his own choices. Marco would always be there to help his little brother, but he no longer needed to feel guilty for José's choices.

Seeing things as they are instead of how we want them to be can be painful. It means seeing hard truths. But it's important to withhold judgments and keep your observation limited to *the present moment.* Make a list of guilt-producing realities in life *right now.*

Focus on how things honestly are now, as painful as it may seem. It's ultimately more liberating to see things as they are, not as you want them to be. And remember that things generally aren't set in stone. For now, just acknowledging the truth is a crucial first step.

I enter each moment with a nonjudgmental
view of reality.

Soothing

Painful feelings like guilt are a natural part of life, but we can learn to control them. In fact, when we ignore our negative emotions they grow and can consume our lives. The trick to helping emotions run their natural course (rather than getting stuck inside us and never resolving themselves) is to acknowledge their existence and their origin, and to soothe them.

For some of us self-soothing is a foreign concept, especially if we weren't soothed as children. If we were ignored or abused or simply misunderstood, it can be particularly challenging to figure out how to soothe ourselves. In *Don't Let Your Emotions Run Your Life*, Scott E. Spradlin describes how many people resort to impulsive behaviors in their desperate but misguided attempts to self-soothe: "They may hit or yell at people they're angry with, or attempt to soothe themselves by overeating, bingeing, overusing alcohol, misusing prescription meds, cutting themselves, and so on. These impulsive behaviors can be successful in momentarily quelling the emotion, but they can become long-standing behavioral responses to emotional crises, and ultimately unhelpful."

This self-destructive behavior, though contradictory, is a pretty common response in our culture. Soothing ourselves in loving, helpful ways requires us to be vulnerable—in a way that hurting others and ourselves does not. And that vulnerability can feel dangerous and terrifying, especially for those of us who've been trained to hide our feelings at all costs. But ultimately these destructive responses only create more problems and leave us with even more unresolved painful feelings.

Building our resources for healthy self-soothing not only helps to ameliorate our pain, it is essential to relinquishing our self-destructive habits. For instance, when we try to quit smoking, drinking in excess, attacking ourselves or others, or when we're trying to let go of excessive and chronic guilt, we must have a positive soothing behavior to replace these destructive soothing behaviors.

EXERCISE

List ways you can imagine soothing yourself uses your five senses (See Spradlin's book for an extensive list of ideas if you find yourself getting stuck). Imagine activities that engage multiple senses, such as soaking in a warm, scented bath while listening to calming music, flipping through a magazine full of pretty pictures of nature, and sipping a cool glass of juice. Also make sure there are plenty of activities you can do in your own home with minimal preparation, since emotional crisis isn't the best time to have to pull together an elaborate plan. Once you've got your list, start using it on a regular basis, engaging in at least one of the activities each time you feel guilty, depressed, anxious, angry, and the like. While the goal isn't to completely banish painful feelings (oftentimes that will require more reflection and possibly positive action), the point is to reassure your deepest self that you care how you feel, that you don't have to suffer through everything, and that your feelings are important and worthy of loving care.

When painful feelings come up, I acknowledge and soothe myself in healthy ways.

Integrity

To be called a person of integrity is one of the highest compliments we could receive. And yet integrity is a quality that is in danger of extinction, in a culture that pushes us to take the faster and easier low road, instead of the more treacherous and cumbersome high road.

In order to act from a place of integrity, we must know ourselves. We must establish our own sense of right and wrong, fair and unfair, loving and unloving. Having integrity means that we don't compromise to avoid pain, conflict, or adversity. We cannot allow our guilt to be our driving force.

In his thoughtful treatise *Integrity*, author and Yale law professor Stephen L. Carter offers a compelling discussion about the connection between guilt and lack of integrity. He uses as one example the ever-increasing problem of grade inflation, in which today's teachers are pressured to make "A" the average grade and "B" a grade for students doing average or even below average work. Carter theorizes that "a good deal of grade inflation probably stems from the desire of professors to avoid the guilty feelings that honest grading might generate, as well as a fear of being disliked by students, or perhaps simply a fear of arguing with them. The net effect is that the grades the students work so hard to earn matter a good deal less."

As Carter's example demonstrates, when we compromise our own integrity, we lower the standards—and thus the ultimate potential—of everyone for whom we compromise our integrity. When teachers and professors, as well as administrators and educational institutions, keep their standards for achievement high, they risk the upset of students, parents, and the community at large. They risk feeling guilty for giving the grade that was actually earned, but in return for that risk they stand to inspire students to try harder, seek more help, and, ultimately, reach the bar that has been raised to the appropriate level.

Integrity means standing up for what you believe is right, while respecting the differing opinions of others. It means setting high standards for yourself and others, and allowing everyone the chance to reach the bar.

Think about one situation in your life in which you aren't acting with full integrity. Whatever it is, it's something that you've been telling yourself "I can't help it," or, "It's just easier this way," even though deep down you know that you're letting yourself down by taking the easy way out.

Once you've identified at least one way you're not acting with integrity, take action to correct it. It's never, ever too late to start acting with integrity from your authentic self. Own up, take responsibility, and raise that bar for yourself and everyone around you. And when you do this, do it with loving kindness toward yourself. This is a chance to support and celebrate yourself, not a reason to criticize past missteps.

I express my true self with authenticity, and I do what's right even when it feels challenging.

SECTION II

Balance

Recognition

There are many approaches to understanding guilt. In her book *Guilt Is the Teacher, Love Is the Lesson*, psychologist and author Joan Borysenko distinguishes between healthy and unhealthy guilt. She explains, "In the state of unhealthy guilt, it is not the omission or commission of a specific act that triggers remorse. Instead, we live in a constant state of diminishment regardless of what we do or don't do." When experiencing unhealthy guilt, people "blame themselves for things that are not their fault, their responsibility, or even their business." Healthy guilt, on the other hand, "teaches us conscience by providing emotional feedback about the consequences of hurtful behavior."

Understanding this distinction—and changing your behavior accordingly—is crucial to achieving a guilt-free life. While most of this book is targeted toward helping you alleviate unhealthy guilt, this chapter can help you gain clarity about which kinds of guilty feelings you have, resolve any healthy guilt from your past, and avoid guilt-warranting behavior in the future.

Healthy Guilt

Guilt is warranted when you:

- Steal something you don't need to survive.
- Speak maliciously about someone you're supposed to care about.
- Use insults or bodily harm to "solve" a conflict of opinions.
- Lie or cheat to come out ahead of others or make yourself "look good."
- Berate, demean, or undermine yourself or others.

Unhealthy Guilt

Guilt is *not* warranted when you:

- Take plenty of time to tend to yourself and enjoy life.
- Ask for a raise or a promotion, or use earned vacation pay or sick days.
- Insist that others treat you with care and respect.
- Express your honest opinions or feelings without trying to change the opinions or feelings of others.
- Enjoy your own good fortunes in life.

Once you're clear about the origins of your guilt, you can start to clean up the existing guilt in your life. Commit to applying respect toward yourself and others in all of your words and actions. Be considerate of the needs and feelings of others *and* yourself. If you live your life by the principles of respect, you will have no cause for guilt in your life.

Make a comprehensive list of all the things in your life you feel guilty about, being as specific and detailed as possible. Then, on a separate sheet of paper, label two columns "Healthy Guilt" and "Unhealthy Guilt." For each item on your list, ask the questions, "Were my actions hurtful? Was this situation truly my responsibility? Did I behave cruelly or disrespectfully?" Only when the honest answer is "yes" should the item be categorized as "Healthy Guilt." In these cases, use the following chapter on "Action" to help you decide on a specific action to take in order to make amends for your disrespectful behavior. (Later, you can apply other exercises in this book to resolve issues of unhealthy guilt.)

I treat others and myself with the utmost respect at all times.

Action

In *The Art of Happiness* by His Holiness the Dalai Lama and Howard C. Cutler M.D., it is explained that, "The Tibetan language doesn't even have an equivalent for the English word "guilt" although it does have words meaning "remorse" or "repentance" or "regret" with a sense of "rectifying things in the future." Rather than spending all of our energy holding on to useless guilt, why not resolve it? Especially when we do something disrespectful that intentionally or thoughtlessly harms someone, we need to do something to rectify the situation.

Lynn works full-time and has two daughters, while her brother-in-law makes enough money for his wife Jade to stay home and live a life of leisure. Yet the responsibilities for the family holidays and celebrations always seemed to fall on Lynn's already burdened shoulders.

Lynn already had some built-up resentment when she called Jade from work one November afternoon to ask if Jade could host the family's yearly Christmas Eve dinner. Jade yawned and said she was too tired to host this year. Angry, Lynn simply said, "Fine," and hung up the phone.

Lynn then launched into a full-blown diatribe about Jade to her coworkers. She mimicked Jade's voice, talking about her spa treatments and cosmetic surgeries, and how *exhausted* they left her. Lynn was blowing off steam, and coworkers laughed along hysterically.

Turned out Lynn hadn't hung up the phone all the way, and Jade had overheard the whole hurtful tirade. Jade called her husband crying, and he called Lynn's husband in a rage. When Lynn got home from work and heard what happened, she was mortified—and awash in dreadful shame and guilt. "I've never felt worse about myself," Lynn said.

Lynn phoned and said, "Look, I hope you can forgive me. I'm jealous, and my behavior was infantile and inexcusable. I *never* should have talked about you like that, and I promise I'll never do it again. You have every right to be furious at me, and I'm really sorry. I hope you'll still spend the holidays with everyone."

Although Jade accepted Lynn's apology, she's refused every holiday invitation since. Lynn could still be guilt ridden and blame herself, but she has a healthier perspective, "I did something awful, and then I did everything I could to make amends. She may never forgive me, but I've had to forgive myself."

Take action to clear up some festering, warranted guilt (first complete the exercise in the "Recognition" chapter). **Contact someone** you hurt, focusing only on *your behavior* and *your regrets* (without tearing yourself down, and without complaining about the other person). If you have no way of contacting them, determine an action you can take to help tip the scales back into balance (volunteer or donate to charity). Then say "I forgive myself," release your guilt, and move on with your life with more respectful intentions. No matter the response from the other person, remember that guilt is an internal emotion, and only you can alleviate and resolve it.

I take responsibility for my actions and own up to my mistakes.

Acceptance

Today, we are expected to "do it all"—work, fun, family, adventure, work, friends, exercise, travel, work, self-care (and did we mention "work"?). Life is a balancing act, and each of us walks a high wire of conflicting desires and responsibilities. Inevitably, things get neglected from time to time. It's easy to find tons of reasons to feel guilty of failure.

Jackie had to walk through the fires of guilt to learn a tough lesson about life balance. She'd hated it when women neglected their friendships for a new love interest. Jackie put a lot of energy into her friendships; she saw them as primary relationships. Yet she often felt abandoned by her newly coupled friends.

Then Jackie herself was swept off her feet. Suddenly, there was someone new in her life taking up several nights a week of her time. Rather than let her friendships lag, though, Jackie continued to see several friends each week—giving up alone time.

"This went on for months," Jackie said, "and I was completely exhausted. Something had to give, but I didn't want to be one of 'those women' I'd complained about."

In the end, Jackie had to accept the reality of the situation: She didn't have as much social time now that she had a thriving love life. At first, this acceptance brought with it waves of guilt; she worried her friends would think she cared about them less. She knew that wasn't true, but it felt like it was.

Then, after much agonizing, Jackie decided to write personal notes to each of her friends about why they were important to her. She wrote, "Even though I've had to accept that I won't be able to hang out quite as often, I care about you and our friendship. I'll always be here for you when you need me, and I'll still make time to enjoy your company and have fun together."

Once she accepted the reality of the situation, Jackie could let go of her guilt and focus more on quality time than on quantity of time. And she was able to embrace someone new and exciting in her life without abandoning herself or those who were precious to her.

EXERCISE

Review the list you made of the sources of your healthy and unhealthy guilt (see "Recognition" chapter). For each item, ask yourself: What reality do I need to accept in order to release my guilt? (For instance, do you need to accept that you have limited time and energy, that you're human and make mistakes, or that it's impossible to please all people all of the time?) Once you've identified the reality associated with your guilty feelings, ask yourself "What can I do to make this reality more bearable?" Like Jackie, you may be able to find a reasonable middle ground that allows you to live fully and guilt-free.

It's okay to set limits and divide my time and energy in a way that feels good to me.

Compassion

Left to your own devices, it's hard enough to let go of guilty feelings. But how do you respond when someone's guilt-tripping you with, "How could you?" or "Who do you think you are?" Do you get angry and dig in your heels, or silently seethe while going along with what they want? Do you succumb to the guilt, believing you've done something hurtful by having your own needs and desires?

When I first met Anna she had a meaningful job, a loving partner, and a thriving community of friends—yet she took little pleasure from life. She was too busy feeling responsible for her elderly parents' unhappiness. She visited them often, but her mother complained that Anna didn't come often enough. When Anna talked about places she'd visited or things she'd done, her dad would say, "Must be nice," or "I wouldn't know. All I do is sit here all day." Her parents' disapproving comments, negativity, and lack of curiosity about her life drained Anna. She felt like a terrible daughter

43

and, at the same time, she felt silently enraged that her parents couldn't manage to find some happiness for her and themselves.

After years of taking on the guilt, a trusted friend suggested that perhaps there was nothing Anna could do to alleviate her parent's unhappiness (though even if there was, their emotions were their responsibility). He suggested that Anna could try to hold compassion in her heart for her parents *and* herself, and start to focus on her own happiness. "It was hard to accept that my guilt wasn't somehow helping my parents. But I had actually been confusing guilt with compassion. I thought if I wasn't guilty, I didn't care," explained Anna.

In *When Things Fall Apart*, Pema Chödrön writes about pairing compassion with our new awarenesses, "The challenge is how to develop compassion right along with clear seeing, how to train in lightening up and cheering up rather than becoming guilt-ridden and more miserable."

Anna's new awareness was that her actions were not alleviating her parents' unhappiness. Rather than falling into despair and hopelessness about that, she let herself off the hook for saving them from themselves and allowed herself to set her regrets aside and just feel compassion and sorrow for them. "I let go of the delusion that I was responsible for causing or fixing their disappointments." Once Anna stopped overcompensating, she was left with tons more energy to enjoy her own life.

Think about a recent incident where you were guilt-tripped. Why did you feel guilty? Do you believe your needs or actions were unacceptable or in conflict with the other person's needs? Now close your eyes and imagine a conversation with the other person and allow your heart to fill with compassion for both of you. Acknowledge their feelings without taking responsibility for them, and then allow yourself to express your own feelings and needs without permission seeking or justification.

I respond to the suffering of others
with compassion.

Communication

When confronted with a guilt-tripper, you have two decisions to make: 1) Will you take on the guilt, and 2) How will you respond?

If you've done something hurtful, then experiencing some healthy guilt can spur you to take reparative action. But if you haven't done anything hurtful and the other person is still handing you a dose of guilt, then you have to refrain from accepting the guilt and decide how best to respond.

Jackson is a committed, passionate third-grade teacher. He loves the kids, but sometimes the parents can be another matter. Recently, Jackson had a particularly difficult run-in with a student's father. While the class was beginning long-division, Colin was still struggling with basic addition and subtraction. Colin was a good kid who tried hard, but he was frustrated and discouraged as the class left him behind. After yet another afternoon watching Colin bite on his pencil and furrow his eyebrows, Jackson decided to call Colin's parents.

Jackson explained to Colin's dad that he was concerned

about Colin. He suggested that Colin might benefit from extra help with his homework, and he recommended a supplemental workbook he had found helpful. But instead of appreciating Jackson's time and concern, Colin's dad laid in with the guilt-tripping. Jackson couldn't believe it. Colin's dad said, "Well, isn't it your job to teach him these things? Where do you get off telling me to do your job for you?"

Jackson hadn't done anything hurtful, so he knew that taking on this father's guilt wouldn't be warranted. "I calmly told Colin's dad that I *am* dedicated to my job and all thirty of my students, but that what Colin needed was practice so he could catch up. I explained that I was calling because I cared about Colin's progress, and that the extra support of his parents or perhaps a tutor was what Colin needed in my professional opinion." Colin's dad groused that he'd "see what he could do." The next week Colin mentioned that he had a great new tutor.

Everyone is different about how they respond to a guilt trip. Sometimes, it may feel best to deal with your guilt internally and just ignore a guilt-tripper. But in Jackson's case, just being silent and letting the situation go would have left Colin without the help he needed. Standing up to Colin's dad had two tangible benefits: Colin got the help he needed, and Jackson maintained his dignity and self-respect.

 EXERCISE

The next time someone tries to force unwarranted responsibility on you, consider the benefit of being direct. Carole Honeychurch and Angela Watrous, in *Talk to Me: Tips for the Small-Talk*

Challenged, suggest a three-part strategy for assertive communication, "Express what you think about a situation, your feelings about a situation, and what you want from a situation." The goal isn't to change the other person's mind, it's to express yourself fully for your own peace of mind.

I can respectfully and honestly express myself to anyone, anytime.

Connection

We're taught to suppress our emotions. Explicit in this is the notion that emotions are weaknesses that should be eliminated or denied. However, left untended, negative feelings don't disappear; they grow. Suppressing our emotions can lead to anger and resentment, despair and depression, and shame and guilt.

Janessa had intense shame about her body, which led to her developing an eating disorder. She privately binged on foods she felt she "shouldn't" eat, especially when she felt upset or stressed, which provided brief pleasure but ultimately left her feeling disgusted with herself and her body. These feelings were among her most painful life experiences, yet she told no one.

Janessa started turning down dates with friends and her boyfriend, preferring to eat in miserable solitude. She felt guilty for missing out on their lives but couldn't stop saying no to their invitations. In time, her friends stopped calling as much, and her boyfriend broke up with her; she believed their actions were a result of their feelings about the way she looked, rather than the way she was acting. Life spun out of control; meals felt like an experience of crime and punishment.

In *Shame and Guilt: Masters of Disguise,* Jane Middleton-Moz lays out the shame/guilt cycle that so many of us experience, "Shame is an isolating feeling. We keep it hidden, yet the more we isolate it . . . the bigger it grows and the lonelier we feel. The more shame we feel, the more internal anger we feel. The greater the anger, the greater the fear of abandonment. We may express the anger or turn it back on ourselves in the form of depression. We feel guilty in an attempt to save our attachment to others. Then, of course, we feel shame all over again."

After several years of depression, Janessa finally recognized she needed help. She found a therapist who led a women's support group around eating issues. At first, Janessa was surprised that the other women were so forthright. But after weeks of encouragement and support, she finally told her story, and when she left that night she felt a tiny bit less awful than she had when she arrived. She was beginning to understand the power of telling her truth.

Consider sharing all or part of your guilt list (from the "Recognition" exercise) with someone you love and trust. Tell this person that you're working on learning how to live a life without guilt, and that part of the process of doing so is examining, processing, and sharing your guilty feelings with others in order to eventually release those feelings. Ask this person to listen without judgments or the pressure to "fix" your guilt. Explain that simply airing your deepest feelings and having them met with love and acceptance is what you hope to achieve in this process (and offer to reciprocate, should they want to make their own list and share it with you).

I find deep connection with others by sharing both my positive and negative feelings.

Love

Have you ever felt like your relationship is a teeter-totter between guilt and resentment? First you're on the ground, feeling guilty because you haven't done enough or given enough to the person you love. So you give to lighten yourself and your guilt. You slowly rise off the ground, and at first it feels good. Until you give "too much," and you start to resent your sweetheart for not reciprocating. Suddenly you're high above the ground, waiting for reciprocation. Your partner now feels obligated to give back, just so they can ascend. Soon giving and receiving feel like calculated obligations instead of generous acts of love.

In their groundbreaking work, *A General Theory of Love,* authors Thomas Lewis, M.D., Fari Amini, M.D., and Richard Lannon, M.D. use scientific research on the human brain to examine how both psychology and biology affect who and why we love. In looking at the fragility of modern relationships, they address this tit-for-tat mentality many succumb to:

"The prevailing myth reaching most contemporary ears is this: *relationships are 50-50.* When one person does a nice thing for the other, he is entitled to an equally pleasing benefit—the sooner the better, under the terms of this erroneous dictum. The physiology of love is no barter. Love is simultaneous and mutual regulation, wherein each person meets the needs of the other, because neither can provide for his own. Such a relationships is *not* 50-50—it's 100-100."

When both people give freely out of love, the balancing act dissolves. Neither feels guilty, because both give 100 percent. Neither feels resentful, because needs are being met. The rewards are abundant: "Each takes perpetual care of the other, and, within concurrent reciprocity, both thrive. For those who attain it, the benefits of deep attachment are powerful—regulated people feel whole, centered, alive ... they are resilient to the stresses of daily life, or even to those of extraordinary circumstance."

EXERCISE

Consider your closest relationship, and imagine what it would look like if it were to become 100-100 instead of 50-50 (or 70-30 or 60-40). What would you be receiving on an ongoing basis? And what would you be giving? How would your life and your relationship transform? Would you have more quality together time, or more alone time, or both? What would it mean if you could both do more for each other, while receiving more from each other? Try to imagine a typical interaction, day, or week with this 100-100 balance. Ask yourself, would I have more or less energy, more or less peace, more or less love? After really allowing your imagination to run wild dreaming up your ideal mutual loving connection, consider asking your loved one to do the same. Then come together, and talk about the possibility of trying out a 100-100 arrangement for a week. With continued commitment and a shared goal of mutuality, you'll have your greatest chance of allowing love to conquer the guilt-resentment cycle, once and for all.

I deserve lovingly mutual relationships in which both people give 100 percent.

Responsibility

Flaking out on your commitments is a sure-fire path to guilt. Are you prone to making promises you know you can't keep (or don't really want to keep)? Do you always feel like you're letting everyone, including yourself, down? Do you feel chronically overstressed and unsuccessful at life? If so, here's your chance to take some responsibility and address the underlying problems behind this guilt bugaboo.

Take Roberto. He loved his partner, Stan, and their young daughter, Julia, very much. He also loved his job as a real estate broker, and the market was hopping. But he found that he was consistently coming into work late, with the words, "sorry" on his lips, because he wanted to help get Julia ready for school. And yet that meant he had to work late, and often on weekends, and he was always apologizing to Stan for how much time he was spending away from their family.

Eager to alleviate his guilt both toward his job and toward his family, Roberto committed to spending more time with both. But this was an unrealistic promise, albeit well-intentioned, and Roberto just kept digging himself in deeper and feeling worse and worse about himself. He got so tired of feeling guilty that he started feeling angry and resentful in both of these very important parts of his life.

Finally, Roberto talked to Stan about his dilemma. Together, they worked out a more realistic plan, where Roberto only helped Julia get ready for school on Monday and Tuesday, his days off. On the other days, he went to work early, before Julia even woke up, but he also stopped scheduling appointments with clients that caused him to get home later than he promised. This allowed him to feel organized and on top of things at work, while still eating dinner every night at home with his family. By taking on a more realistic set of responsibilities and sticking to them, Roberto actually felt more responsible, and his guilt and resentment melted away.

EXERCISE

Start making weekly lists of everything you commit to with your time and energy. At the end of the week, put a check mark next to every responsibility you feel you've adequately addressed (that is, you feel genuinely good about your relationship to that commitment and you feel that you've honored it fully). If there are a good number of items (or some especially important items) that don't have check marks, try to commit to slightly less the following week, so your energy isn't spread as thin. Keep up this process until you can honestly put check marks next to all or almost all of the items on your list. If you have trouble lessening your responsibilities, try to remember that it feels much better to honor a more reasonable amount of commitments than it does to flake on a ton of responsibilities.

I come through on my promises and commitments, and I only make promises and commitments that I can keep.

Appreciation

When we feel guilty for everything we're not doing (or not doing perfectly), we feel bad inside. We often resent the people or situations that "make" us feel guilty. We ruminate on other's faults, accusing, "Hey, you're not so great, either, buddy!" Trouble is, this spiral of criticism and blame is never resolved. In the game of "Who's worst?" everybody loses.

Barb is the sole accountant at a start-up high-tech company. This was the first job in which she wasn't being supervised by more experienced accountants, and she was riddled with insecurities: She wondered, "What if I mess up? Everyone's job is counting on me balancing the books and making sure our cash flow can keep up with our research and production. If I blow it, I could lead to the ruin of the whole company."

As the company grew, so did the pressure. Barb started scrutinizing everyone's decisions. If one of their mistakes led to her not having enough money to be able to pay the bills, she reasoned, then the guilt of the failure would be on their shoulders, not hers. Finding blame for the potential demise of her company reached obsessive proportions; her fellow employees were put off by her snide comments and nervous attitude.

In *The Path to Love,* Deepak Chopra recommends looking at your own perceived faults as a path to appreciating your gifts and those of others: "Engaging in the habit of criticism only postpones the day when your own secret judgments come to light. Bringing to light whatever you think is wrong about yourself is the only way to diffuse guilt and shame." Chopra encourages readers to look at our perceived faults not as an opportunity to beat up on ourselves, but rather as an opportunity to acknowledge the truth of our fears and feelings and meet them with love, compassion, and reason. He hopes that this approach will allow us to see the real truth, "In reality, there is nothing wrong with you or anyone else."

In order to stop the cycle of blame and guilt that was causing Barb and her coworkers misery, Barb had to own up to her fears of inadequacy. She then had to focus on her own performance instead of that of others, and allow that she and her coworkers would succeed or fail together; as long as they all put in positive effort, they'd have no valid cause for guilt no matter the ultimate outcome.

EXERCISE

List your self-criticisms, especially the ones related to your guilty feelings (you may find your list of healthy and unhealthy guilt from the

"Recognition" chapter to be a useful starting point). Then, for each one, try to find some way to appreciate that part of yourself. For example, appreciate that your anger forces you to stand up for injustice. Appreciate your emotions, including your negative ones, for the information they provide you, and start taking positive actions based on that invaluable information.

I appreciate the intrinsic goodness in myself and every human being.

Transformation

It can be tempting to try to deny, ignore, hide, or run from our negative feelings. The trouble is, unless our guilt, anger, resentment, jealousy, and sadness are acknowledged and addressed, they will only grow stronger. So, in order to achieve a guilt-free life, we must first walk into the face of guilt and confront our guilty feelings head-on.

Jonathan is a Vietnam veteran who suffers from "survivor guilt." This kind of guilt is common for those who survive or escape a situation that inflicts death or extreme pain and suffering on others. For more than twenty years, Jonathan avoided his painful feelings about his war experience. He was depressed and homeless, long-since disconnected from family and friends, and he drank and used drugs to avoid his intensely painful guilt about surviving a war that took many lives.

It wasn't until a shelter worker offered to drive Jonathan to a veteran support group that Jonathan finally started facing his guilty feelings. In the company of others who shared his pain, he was able to admit over time to feeling both guilty and relieved that it wasn't he who died. For Jonathan, this was a first step in recovering from his pain and moving on with his life. From there, he began taking free meditation classes at the veteran's center, where he was also assisted in getting clean and off the streets.

In his book *Peace in Every Step,* author Thich Nat Hanh offers the following five-step process to transforming feelings: "Recognize each feeling as it arises . . . become one with the feeling . . . calm the feeling . . . release the feeling . . . [and] look deeply . . . by looking, you will see what will begin to help you transform the feeling."

Over several years, Jonathan was able to resolve his survivor guilt, which made space for his intense sadness and grief to surface. Our emotional self is like an onion—peel away one feeling and another is always there to follow it. His journey was not an easy or simple one. But he was able to use the same meditation techniques to tend to his ongoing pain, and this allowed him to again find a degree of peace in his life.

The next time you feel guilty, allow yourself to name that feeling. See where you feel it most in your body, and name the sensations (for example, cringing in your face, tightness in your chest, tension in your back or stomach). Sit with the awareness of those physical sensations and emotions, while you allow yourself to breathe in and out. Speak soothingly to the feeling, and once you begin to feel calmer silently repeat to yourself, "Let go, let go, let go" with each breath. Then "look deeply," and investigate the originating circumstances of the guilty feeling. If your guilt is of a healthy origin (that is, if it was caused by your own hurtful actions), take action to resolve the situation.

I turn toward all of my feelings and soothe them.

Joy

Passion

Do you remember how you answered the question, "What would you like to be when you grow up?" Do you also remember what stood in your way?

Judith Kaye entered the workforce in the 1960s. She was a budding, enthusiastic journalist, but opportunities for women in this profession were close to nil at the time. Undeterred, she began working at a small, local paper while going to night school to get her law degree. Again, she faced an unsupportive atmosphere and was plagued by the simple fact that there were so few women doing what she fervently wanted to do. Predictably, her colleagues challenged her dedication by pitting her work against her family, often making her choose between the two to prove her dedication. Due to her perseverance and ability to say, "I deserve this," Judith secured a position at a prestigious law firm, eventually becoming the first woman to occupy the top judicial office of New York State.

As difficult as it was to forge a path for women to hold important, challenging positions, she wondered how those closest to her were affected by her choices. What did her husband and children have to give up in order for her to pursue what she loved? She finally had to develop a resilient response to the nagging thought that she was being selfish. She had to remind herself that men aren't forced to choose between family and career, and that she didn't have to either. She had to remain true to her passion.

Our passions develop naturally as we learn what drives us. But invariably, our fears bubble up or other people try to dissuade us. Often our choices are based on how others feel about our pursuits, rather than on our placing ultimate importance on how we'll suffer if we give up our life's passion. But suppressing our desires in the recesses of our mind extinguishes our enthusiasm for life. There remains a vital part of us that hungers to unearth them and offer up our true gifts to our families and communities.

Accepting ourselves and following our passions isn't just a selfish act—it also sets a tremendous example to those around us. Judith's granddaughter has something to say about this. When asked what she wants to be when she grows up, the eight-year-old precociously responded, "I'll just be a Supreme Court Judge since that's what Grandma does."

EXERCISE

Reflect on activities that ignite a fire in you. What leaves you so excited you can't wait to share and relive your experiences? What do you enjoy so much that you don't have to feign enthusiasm? Once you've identified your passions, make appointments with yourself each week to pursue them. It may take time and perseverance, and no one else may understand why you care so much. But it's okay, just let yourself linger in your passionate enjoyment and the external rewards and validation will come when they come.

I deserve to nurture my passions and pursue my dreams.

Pleasure

L ife's responsibilities and complexities have a way of causing us to lose touch with life's thrills and surprises. Are
you at a place where you consider pleasure a bonus, something you need to earn or withhold depending on your pro-
ductivity and success? Do pleasurable activities feel like an
indulgence, more for special occasions than for the everyday?
Or, if you do allow yourself those things that bring you pleasure, do you find that guilty feelings crop up, along with internal voices that say you're undeserving, spoiled, or selfish? If
so, you aren't alone. Many of us are plagued by cultural mes-
sages that doing things that feel good, just for the fun of it, is
irresponsible and self-indulgent. When Lydia's teenage children told her she needed to take a vacation, she laughed.
Lydia hadn't taken a long weekend for herself, let alone a
vacation, in seventeen years. Her children couldn't remember
the last time she treated herself to anything. How could she
possibly go on a vacation with all the bills to pay? And what
about her work and family responsibilities? But once they

made the suggestion, she found she couldn't stop thinking about a vacation. She started to get in touch with her deep down longings, the ones she'd silenced for way too long, the ones that expressed her need to relax and replenish.

In her book, *Finding Pleasure Everywhere,* SARK reveals, "Pleasure and joy invite our best selves out to play and quiet our critical voices. They give us a much-needed place to creatively refill." It's sad that many of us have forgotten how to play, as if doing so is only suitable for children.

What is life, though, without reveling in the things we delight in most? Pleasure should not be parceled out stingily and sparingly. It's an essential facet of our overall well-being. It's important that you allow yourself to do the things that bring you peace, whether you take pleasure in dreamily staring into space for an hour or hiking to the top of a mountain. Feel your spirits lift and your body awaken the minute you let your senses take over your mind. Feel yourself come alive when you take time to ask yourself what you would truly enjoy in this moment and as you allow yourself to find the satisfaction that you've been craving.

Make a "pleasures list" for yourself, including up to one hundred things you truly enjoy. **An ice cream cone on a hot day, cuddling with your cat, taking naps, snapping photos, tending to the yard, taking the guided tour at a museum, reading a book in the park**—these are just some small pleasures to get you started. Once you have your list, start integrating those pleasures into your everyday life. Even on busy days, try to find time to sing along with the radio or call your best friend (or whatever it is that you can do to add a splash of pleasure into your day!).

I deserve and enjoy all the pleasures life offers.

Focus

Ralph Waldo Emerson said, "Most of the shadows of this life are caused by standing in one's own sunshine." What are the sources of light that come from within you? (What are your brightest qualities, talents, gifts?) And what's blocking your light from shining forth?

One of Serena's sources of sunshine was her creativity. She started a small home business selling her unique handmade jewelry, focusing her attention on bringing her vision to light. But self-doubt and regret often crowded out the thrill of pursuing this new career. Her day job at a coffee shop left her with plenty of time to let her mind wander, and rather than wander to her dreams, it wandered to her fears. Was she growing her business fast enough? Would it ever be profitable enough to support her?

Serena was sacrificing a lot to support this dream. Her boyfriend and friends complained they never saw her. She felt riddled with guilt, yet she couldn't fathom letting go of her new business. In addition, her internal conflicts about what she was giving up to pursue her dream left her feeling foggy, disoriented, and confused.

One day a customer at the café started a conversation about Serena's jewelry. The customer, an entrepreneur herself, offered to help Serena with a business plan, including a strategy for integrating her social life into her work life and a target for slowly scaling back her hours at the café until the business was her full-time gig.

Serena shared her plan with the people she loved, asking for support and understanding. She started a monthly potluck for her friends; Saturdays were devoted to her boyfriend. And she took one evening a week to relax and rejuvenate on her own. After a year of hard work and sacrifice, Serena finally built up enough steady clients to allow her to quit her day job and focus on her business full-time. She felt lucky to be doing something she loved, surrounded by what she lovingly created. Her intense focus had made her sun shine right through the clouds.

EXERCISE Spend an hour focusing on your ideal life. Write down what it would look like: What would you be doing that would bring you vitality and satisfaction, what would your most important relationships be like? This isn't a fantasy trip about winning the lottery; this is a chance to focus your attention on your dreams, hopes, and aspirations. You'll know you're on the right track when you feel grounded, excited, and hopeful. Once you get that out on paper, write out a business plan, breaking your bigger goals down into manageable pieces. For example, if you dream of being a physical therapist, include "researching programs," "applying to school," "attending school," and other small steps to establishing your business. Then take the first step in each of your plans. Now is the time to focus your love and energy in the direction you want to head.

I focus my attention and energies on what brings forth my inner light.

Independence

Natasha was the friend who will never let anyone down and was always willing to come to the rescue. She listened to problems and provided advice, empathy, and support. But she ignored the management of her own life. She celebrated other's successes, but her own dreams languished. She suffered with them during hard times, though she had some long-unresolved grief of her own. She lost connection with herself.

In Robin Norwood's *Daily Meditations for Women Who Love Too Much,* she explains, "When we feel responsible for another's behavior and we cannot bear our own guilt and anguish, we need help managing our own uncomfortable feelings, not help managing that other person's life." Taking personal responsibility heightens our sense of self-efficacy and self-confidence. And allowing others to do the same for themselves shows ultimate love and respect. It also allows us to enjoy healthier relationships.

When Natasha learned how to channel a majority of her energy toward herself, she felt whole. She asked for and received a long overdue promotion. She started journaling as a way to purge her long-ignored pain. She felt more in control, and, ironically, more connected. She realized that her friends still loved her just as much. She felt guilty the first time she said "no" (close friends had asked her to help them move on a weekend during which she'd planned a solo spa date), so she wrote down her feelings in her journal, and then let her massage therapist rub any lingering concerns away. At the end of the weekend, she was refreshed enough to bring over a pizza to her friends' new abode—something she genuinely wanted to do.

Focusing on our own needs can be a challenge for many of us, especially if we're used to judging our self-worth on how much we're connected to others or how much we help them out, or if we constantly compare ourselves to others as a way to see if we're okay or not. We need instead to consciously step away on a regular basis and listen for our own inner, authentic voice; getting in touch with how we *really* feel and think through this kind of thoughtful, concentrated practice will develop a kind of independence that allows us to love and connect, one whole human being to another.

Plan a weekly solo date night. **Dine at a restaurant you've been meaning to try, go see that quirky film, or run yourself a nice bath and crank up your favorite tunes. Spending time alone can be challenging at first; with no one there to distract you, you may find that all kinds of negative or guilty thoughts pop up. Just give those thoughts their due attention (ignoring them only makes them stronger), and then soothe yourself with comforting and reassuring words. During these evenings, and as often as possible, focus your energy on treating yourself as you would your best friend.**

I take strength and comfort from
my independence.

Poise

To become our most powerful selves, we must learn how to advocate for ourselves rather than to tear ourselves down. We should prioritize our emotional, intellectual, physical, and spiritual needs, allowing our confidence to grow. By redirecting our critical tendencies, and acting from a place of centered authenticity rather than acting out our own insecurities, we become individuals who are infectiously positive, genuine, and confident. We can then take on a self-assured quality that allows us to tackle daily battles with grace and poise.

When Pua arrived at Maria's office for lunch, she found Maria in the midst of a difficult phone meeting. The man she was speaking to was yelling loudly through the phone. By the time the call ended, the man's hostile behavior had overcome Maria. She stomped around her office, barking with disbelief that such a person could exist, carrying on in her righteousness. Pua listened intently and patiently, and then, raising her hands up as if making an offering to the Gods, she responded "Lift him up."

Pua's soothing tone and poise made Maria pause, take a breath, and wrap her arms around herself. Pua's centered manner helped Maria realize she was shaking, and shouting, and that her body was charged with the man's negativity. She had internalized the situation and his attitude. Meanwhile, Pua was looking at her with gentle, compassionate eyes, accepting the imperfections of both Maria and the man.

Because Maria placed a negative judgment on the man, she reacted personally to the situation, rather than with detachment like Pua. When the inner judgmental critic controls us, we and those around us are constantly falling short of unrealistic ideals. And when we project these ideals onto others, we ironically fail to live up to our own expectations. It's easier to feel guilty than to face the fact that we are flawed, ordinary people. When we set ourselves up for the unattainable, this guilt chips away at our self-esteem and our ability to live truthfully with others.

Replace that inner critic, with inner poise. In *Becoming a Goddess of Inner Poise*, Donna Freitas states, "Inner Poise does not have to be about becoming perfect . . . Instead, (it) leaves room for loving the self; it includes room for forgiveness when we fall short of our hopes and makes room for new desires to flourish within us."

Truth is, we are all flawed and reacting with grace to any given situation is not easy. But when you learn to love yourself and life while maintaining a healthy respect for others, this translates into an appealing confidence no one can take away from you.

Remember the last time you jumped on the gossip bandwagon with friends or colleagues. This may seem harmless, but it's probably disrespectful and unkind. Imagine how the person would feel if they heard what you were saying and also ask yourself the benefit of the conversation. Next time, practice restraint from judgment and walk away.

I can call on my natural inner poise whenever I need it.

Motivation

Finding the Wind for Your Sails

For the past year, Katie has been learning how to windsurf, yet every Saturday before her class she finds herself listing all the reasons she shouldn't go: It's exhausting, it's expensive, and I'll never be good enough to make it worth the effort, anyway. Then, just as these beliefs start to sink in, she feels the guilt coming on—guilt about wanting to give up, guilt about lacking self-discipline. It's no wonder she finds herself hiding under her blankets, wishing she had never even signed up for the class in the first place.

The key to motivation, whether it's regarding something small or life changing, is focusing on the positive incentives that inspire us to act rather than on all of the possible negative outcomes. In his book *The Now Method*, Neil Fiore describes these two forms of motivation as the "push" and "pull" methods. The push method stimulates action through fear, focusing on an escape from the consequences. The pull method suggests that when we are properly rewarded for our efforts, we can come alive with even the most difficult of tasks. The more immediate and specific the reward, the more likely you will feel motivated to act.

In Katie's case, what she needed was to refocus her attention on the reasons she started windsurfing in the first place: She wanted to learn something that would push her limits, she loves the way her body and mind feel energized at the end of the lesson, and she gets excited with each little bit of progress she makes. Most importantly, she delights in the thrill of gliding on water—even if she's only going ten miles per hour. As soon as she imagines this incredible feeling, she suddenly finds herself getting out of bed and getting ready for class.

EXERCISE

Write a list of five things you wish you could do, but that feel elusive because they take too much time, energy, or risk. The list can range from small things like talking your dog to the park after dinner each night, to transitioning to an entirely new career. Next to each item, log all of the positive outcomes and benefits that could come from fulfilling the goal. For example: If I take my dog to the park each night, she'll be happier and healthier, I'll feel proud of myself for taking good care of her, I'll get some fresh air and exercise, and I'll feel stronger and more energized.

Identifying and then repeatedly focusing on the positive outcomes of your short- and long-term dreams, goals, and aspirations will help build the motivation you need to fuel your steps in the right direction. Use your list as inspiration to start engaging in the things that make you happy.

I focus on the positive rewards of achieving my goals.

Individuality

In a culture steeped with pressure to have the right posses-
sions, relationship, job, body, and friends, we can forget
that each of us must define "right" for ourselves. When we
succumb to the onslaught of Madison Avenue messaging
we're confronted with everyday, we start to believe we have to
conform in order to be seen as successful. But when we
compromise our genuine selves, we set ourselves up for disappointment, regret, and confusion.

Alice was about to graduate high school and was torn
about what to do next. Her friends were all planning to attend
college. But Alice was never able to sit still in school, and
although she was extremely bright, she had difficulty
absorbing the material in the way it was presented to her.
Then her parents posed the question to her, "Would you like
to go to college or use the money for something else?"

She was shocked they would ask such a question,
immediately assuming they didn't believe in her and that she
had let them down. What else could she possibly do with the

money but go to school? Her parents then explained that they didn't want to pressure her into doing something that didn't feel right; they urged her to step outside what her friends were doing and examine her dreams.

Suddenly, the world opened up to Alice. She had an entrepreneurial spirit and decided to use the money to take a handful of business classes. Within a year of her high school graduation, she opened her own consignment shop. After five years in business, and at the tender age of twenty-four, the shop is far exceeding her personal and financial expectations.

Exploring our individuality can be a lonely, unfamiliar journey no matter what our age. Many of us have spent years trying our best to fit in, so the idea of breaking the mold can feel scary and even undesirable. The potential gains of taking this risk, however, are true satisfaction, high self-esteem and genuine fulfillment. As we come into our own and experiment with what feels right, whether it be the clothing we wear or the path we choose in life, we learn the meaning of the phrase, "That is so 'me.'"

EXERCISE

Identifying the unique combination of traits that make you is key to helping you find your true gifts and purpose. What are your nonnegotiable qualities and traits—the things you couldn't and shouldn't change even if you wanted to, even if someone else told you to? Are you sensitive, inquisitive and curious, or strong willed? In your journal, create a nonjudgmental list that defines your individuality. Are you cool and calm or fiery and fierce? Allow yourself to discover who you really are, and then make choices in your life that support and reward your true self (rather than compressing and bending to fit into someone else's ideal).

I am my most powerful self when I am fearlessly me.

Energy

Margie prided herself on her giving nature; she gave to friends, family, and charities. But she neglected her own needs. She ended each day passed out on her couch, exhausted. *Balance* was not part of her vocabulary. She felt plagued with guilt whenever she gave anything less than 150 percent. She couldn't let anyone down, she never paused for self-care, and her energy level plummeted. Finally, when she got a terrible head cold for the third time in as many months, she realized it was time to pause and reevaluate her choices. But what to give up? Every person, every cause felt equally needy of her time and energy.

In *Positive Energy*, Judith Orlaff writes, "Soulful giving is a way of nurturing yourself, and enlarging your capacity to be more caring to people; it's restorative sharing from your heart, never forced. In contrast, codependent giving bleeds life force, is driven by obligation, guilt, or a martyr-complex, conscious or not. It leaves the giver feeling sucked dry, unappreciated, put upon."

Margie's giving was not so much from her heart as from her head. She was on a one-woman crusade to save the world, even while she herself was drowning. She came to realize that she had to develop a habit of nurturing herself. One day every couple of months wasn't enough. She needed to develop a regular practice of recharging her batteries in order to have the energy to do everything she wanted.

Why do so many of us neglect ourselves? Even when we're stressed and run down, we still continue to put everything and everyone else first. Maybe we're waiting for permission—for someone to notice how depleted we are and urge us to do something about it. If we were forced to take care of ourselves, we wouldn't have to confront our familiar companion—guilt. But no one is going to refill your tank but you. Not because they don't care, but because you're the only one with the power to do so. And rather than repeatedly running out of gas and having to hike to the station with a gas can, wouldn't it be easier and much less stressful to fill-up before you're on "E"?

Remember that life is about choices. If you find yourself saying you *have to* do this or that, remember that the reality is that you *choose to*. Be conscious of your choices and the motivation behind them. The energy you have to offer to yourself and others depends on it.

Think about the last time you felt depleted. Looking back, were there physical, mental, and spiritual signs you ignored? For example, a physical sign might be problems sleeping, a mental sign might be a short temper or difficulty concentrating, and a spiritual sign might be depression. Create a list for each category that is personal to you, refer to it regularly, and be responsible for your self-care.

I feel alive and vital, as I am willing and able to care for myself every day.

Delight

Every morning on her way to work, Jane feels consumed with her mental to-do list, which seems never-ending and at times crushing. And then, like clockwork, something happens that brings her perpetual delight: She passes the same elderly Asian man she sees every morning, leisurely riding his bicycle along the tree-lined road. Under his big straw hat, he seems to glow from within. He always looks so at peace with the world and at ease with himself that Jane feels positively enamored with him. But what captivates her most about this routine passing is the handmade cardboard sign he's attached to the front of his basket that reads "God Bless You." She pictures him carefully making the sign, and imagines that he spends his day contentedly riding around spreading his quiet offering of kindness. While she's never spoken to him, he brings her such delight, just through his way of being in the world.

We each have tiny, personal moments that we can either ignore or relish: When our dog uses the top of our foot for a pillow and we can't bear to move. When a stranger strikes up a pleasant conversation with us while in line at the grocery store. When something comical occurs to us and there's no one around to enjoy the joke but ourselves. By paying attention to these moments, rather than brushing over them in a rush to "bigger" things, your life will become an accumulation of truly delightful and meaningful moments.

In Eckhart Tolle's book *The Power of Now,* he offers a very simple strategy, "Forget about your life situation and pay attention to your life." He is referring to the way that we tend to function in the past and the future—with all the guilt, expectations, and confusion they create—rather than living fully in the present. Instead, he entreats us to see, feel, and hear without judgment or analysis. Because when we don't, we become slaves to our criticisms, forever waiting for the day when the good part of our lives will begin.

EXERCISE

Find a place to be—in your home, in nature, or your local coffeehouse—and practice using your senses to experience your surroundings. Write down what you see, hear, and feel, paying special attention to what pleases you. If you start to slip into planning ("I should vacuum that rug") or interpretation ("He must be smiling at me because he wants something") or judgment ("It's too noisy in here"), just notice that tendency without further judgment (there's nothing worse than judging yourself for being judgmental!). Then gently bring your attention back to observing the abundant pleasures and delights in your midst.

Every day I notice and embrace the little things that delight me.

Freedom

In order to release guilt and completely, we must fully love and accept ourselves just as we are. And when we come to this place of self-surrendering, we must learn to not sabotage the freedom it brings by giving in to fear or pressure. Our beauty lies in the nuances of our individuality, and freedom comes from truly exposing and expressing our unique selves—despite what society, family, or culture may say about us.

When Alma contemplated trading her cosmopolitan, modern life in the city for the simplicity of Maui, she did what many do when they're afraid to face what they already know they want—she listed the pros and cons. She scribbled, "playing in nature ... valuing a balanced life ... thrill of a new beginning...." When it came to writing her cons list, the typical fears of a bold move such as finding work or having enough money never crossed her mind. She only had one word for that list: family.

As a first generation Filipina-American, the sacrifices her parents endured sat perched on her shoulder like a little bird reminding her of the good fortune and prosperity she enjoyed as a result. She knew that her moving would be seen as worse than a selfish act; it would be felt as a disappointment and betrayal. She was already the daughter who didn't call or visit enough, the one who chose to study English over the more practical career of nursing. She already experienced first-generation guilt. How could she possibly contemplate doing something that would increase her guilt all the more?

But in the end, she did decide to move, and it was the very thing her parents had instilled in her from the beginning that convinced her to leave—the confidence to be who she is with no apology attached. And as much as she missed them, breaking away ultimately allowed her to better understand and share their experience. Like them, she decided to move far away from everything and everyone she knew. They left in search of opportunity, to thrive from all the possibilities, and experience the ultimate dream—the chance to fully live, in an environment where they felt they could shine. By example, they had shown her how to achieve personal freedom.

In *Freedom,* writer and spiritual teacher Osho advises, "Accept the responsibility of being yourself as you are, with all that is good and with all that is bad, with all that is beautiful and that which is not beautiful. In that acceptance a transcendence happens and one becomes free." It is a challenge to come to this place in our lives, but you can get there with self-care, balance, and joy—and some other words in between.

Choose a recent occasion where you felt like your most powerful self. Write a journal entry about it and the feelings it gave you. Nurture your courage and self-confidence by making this a daily exercise.

I am free to be my most powerful self.

Innocence

Innocence. Contemplate the lightness, the buoyancy of this word. Wrap it around your shoulders. Try it on for size.

When we lose sight of our innocence and instead feel guilty, we can become imprisoned, heavy, and burdened. All too often, we play judge and jury to our own spirit. We find ourselves guilty of being imperfect, and make no allowances for being human. We indict ourselves for having needs, wants, and desires. We sentence ourselves to a lifetime of guilt just for being ourselves.

It's time for an appeal, on the grounds of a mistrial:

When you go to work to support yourself and your family, you're innocent.

When you stay home to care for yourself and your family, you're innocent.

When you honestly speak from your heart, with the intention to connect rather than destroy, you're innocent.

When you ask for what you need, you're innocent.

When you speak out and act up, you're innocent.

Innocent. Innocent. Innocent.

When it comes down to it, each and every one of us on the planet is innocent at our core. Sometimes, in the worst cases, we are wounded and we lash out in all of our fear and anguish. Still, every single one of us is comprised of an innocent essence. At heart, we are all seeking love and connection, acceptance and freedom.

The next time you find yourself on trial, prosecuting yourself for not being everything to everyone, punishing yourself for the blessings in your life, imagine your innocent self walking into the courtroom, coming on to the stand, and simply radiating all of the love and hopes and good intentions inside you. Allow that radiating innocence to wash over your prosecutor, your jury, your judge, your defendant, until you're all united in forgiveness, acceptance, and appreciation. Allow the new verdict to come forth: Not guilty. Innocent at heart, innocent in spirit.

EXERCISE

Go out and play, freeing your innocent spirit. Take a walk, get out into nature, enjoy a friend's company. Celebrate your official relinquishing of guilt.

I am an innocent, loving, and
well-intentioned person.